true green

# true green

## 100 everyday ways you can contribute to a healthier planet

ABC Books

Kim McKay and Jenny Bonnin

Published by ABC Books for the
AUSTRALIAN BROADCASTING CORPORATION
GPO Box 9994 Sydney NSW 2001

*First published November 2006*

ISBN 10: 0 7333 1564 X
ISBN 13: 978 0 7333 1564 0

*Design, layout and select images by Marian Kyte*
*Edited by Tim Wallace*
*Colour reproduction by Graphic Print Group, Adelaide*
*Printed in China by Everbest Printing*

5 4 3 2 1

A percentage of proceeds from the sale of *True Green*
benefits Clean Up Australia.

True Green is a pending Trademark of True Green (Global) Pty Ltd

The paper used to print this book is manufactured from natural,
recyclable products made from wood grown in sustainable forests.

# contents

Australia really is a very lucky country. We are blessed with a natural environment unlike anywhere else and Australians understand and care about it because they know how easily it could be lost or damaged.

I have been lucky enough to see just how much Australians care for their environment through the extraordinary efforts ordinary people make on Clean Up Australia Day. Since 1989, millions of Australians have shown that looking after our country matters. Getting involved and taking action has also prompted this book because we face a major challenge over changes to our climate.

The world's climate is changing more dramatically than we would have believed even a year or two ago. It's no longer a prediction. The evidence is real and unless we do something now, the changes will be significant and damaging.

The good news is that we can do something about climate change. This doesn't mean we have to sacrifice the lifestyles we enjoy now. I believe that the changes necessary are easy to achieve and simple to do. I hope you will join with me in taking those easy steps to save our environment and our planet for our future and our children.

But what does this all have to do with Clean Up Australia? Clean Up inspires and works with communities here in Australia and all around the world, to clean up, fix up and conserve our environment. We help people learn about and understand issues, how every one of us is responsible for the environment and how, through simple actions, we can all make a difference.

Compiled by Clean Up co-founder Kim McKay and fellow director Jenny Bonnin, *True Green: 100 everyday ways you can contribute to a healthier planet* gives you and me, in true Clean Up style, the tools to start taking simple actions today – in our homes, at work and while we're out and about enjoying all the benefits of living in the best country in the world. *True Green* will help get us all on track.

As an added bonus a percentage of the proceeds from the sale of this book are being donated to Clean Up Australia to help us expand the scope and reach of our water and waste campaigns.

If you'd like to get more involved, you can join us by becoming a True Green supporter. Simply go to our website www.cleanup.com.au and sign up today.

So how can you get started?

My tip, choose the top 10 changes you'll make today and then work your way up to more next week, the following week and the weeks after that. It's simple, it's fun, it's rewarding – because every action we select does make a difference.

Aussies have shown just how true blue we are through events like Clean Up Australia Day – now's your chance to do something every day of the year by being true green.

# introduction

Kim McKay and Jenny Bonnin

Every day we read in the newspapers or see on television reports about global warming and climate change. There seems to be a cascade of information and differing scientific opinions. What are we to believe and, more importantly, what can we do?

The vast majority of the world's leading scientists and experts, save for a few contrarians usually supported by industry-funded 'think tanks' and out-of-step politicians, agree that global warming is a reality. The real question facing all of us is how to live with the effects of climate change and minimise its future impact.

In Australia we are already seeing the impact of global warming through the extended drought across much of the country, with water restrictions being imposed on residents of many large cities.

The town of Goulburn, in southern New South Wales, may become one of the first cities in Australia to fully recycle its water due to drought, even though much larger cities like London (which has half the annual rainfall of Sydney) have been doing this for more than 100 years. Our water and environmental management, in this, the driest inhabited continent on earth, lags way behind other developed countries.

But global warming is affecting us in other ways too. Tim Flannery, author of *The Weather Makers*, says the Australian continent will be first and worst-affected by climate change, with the loss of our greatest natural and tourism assets. The casualties of global warming will include losing up to half our rich biodiversity, destruction of the Great Barrier Reef and infiltration of salt water into Kakadu.

As a nation we have no choice but to look for alternate power sources to fossil fuels. There is no time for complacency; we need to look immediately at developing renewable energy sources like solar and wind power – of which Australia has an abundance – to feed our energy needs.

The solution lies with all of us.

When we helped establish Clean Up Australia back in the late 1980s it was in response to a collective frustration evident in the local community. Why were our waterways choked with non-degradable consumer waste products and why was raw sewage flowing freely onto our beaches?

More than 40,000 Sydney-siders, many from the far-western suburbs, converged on the harbour and removed more than 5,000 tonnes of rubbish – including 3,000 used syringes – from our most famed waterway.

While it was a shock to discover the extent to which the harbour had been used as a rubbish tip, it was also incredibly exciting and inspiring to learn first-hand that collective community action can change things. Today, due to the efforts of hundreds of thousands of Clean Up Australia Day volunteers, the harbour and  many other iconic locations are cleaner and better protected.

That same tide of public concern is evident again. We believe we're about to ride a new wave of community action in support of the environment.

True Green is in response to this. Every Australian can make a positive difference to the environment by making simple changes to their lifestyle. You may not be able to do all 100 tips at first but why not set your family a challenge to do 10, then try another 10, then another 10.  Soon you'll be making a real impact. Encourage your neighbours and friends to join you, and involve your family – it's their environment, their health and lifestyle that's at stake.

Have fun, let us know if you have other ideas, and make True Green and Clean Up's goals for a sustainable Australia part of your everyday life.

# you can make a difference

Australians have, on a per capita basis, the highest greenhouse gas emissions of any country in the developed world – hardly an auspicious position for a continent with so much to lose from global warming. The best we've done to redress this is to limit the rate at which emissions are increasing. It's not just the fault of big business – after all, our affluent lifestyles are built on the economic benefits of cheap power from greenhouse-polluting coal and export dollars derived from energy-intensive primary industries. Households contribute almost one-fifth of Australia's greenhouse gases – about 15 tonnes of carbon dioxide per household each year – and much of that can be avoided through the simple steps outlined in this book. Start today. Decide to follow these simple suggestions and immediately reduce your ecological footprint.

The average Australian household produces 15 tonnes of greenhouse gases, uses 230,000 litres of water and creates 1.7 tonnes of landfill waste every year.

# in the home

# 1 reduce

Houses, televisions, meals – as things get bigger so do the demands on the earth. The average Australian's ecological footprint (the area of land required to sustain consumption and waste) is seven hectares – 3.5 times more than what is sustainable globally. We can easily reduce our footprint by avoiding unnecessary consumption. Do you boil enough water for six cups of tea when you want only one? Do you leave the TV or stereo on when you leave the room? Do you throw things away unused? Small acts like this seem insignificant but collectively they add up and contribute to global warming.

- Less waste
- Less pollution
- Lower carbon emissions
- Save money

Image © APL

# reuse 2

M ost of what we consume ends up as rubbish within months, weeks, days or even minutes. Australia is the second-most wasteful society, per capita, in the world after the United States, sending an average of nearly 700 kilograms of waste per person to landfill every year. That's enough rubbish to cover the entire state of Victoria. By extending the life cycle of products we can cut down on that rubbish. Try to buy items that are reusable or come in reusable packaging – and make sure you reuse them. Before you throw it away, ask yourself if that wrapping paper can be saved, that container refilled, that pair of shoes mended or that machine fixed.

- Less waste
- Less pollution
- Lower carbon emissions
- Save money

# 3 recycle

Kerbside recycling programs mean we now recycle more than 1.4 billion glass bottles, 2.3 billion aluminium cans and billions more plastic and paper items every year. Recycling reduces landfill and saves resources: recycling an aluminium can uses only 5 per cent of the energy required to make a new one, recycling glass uses 26 per cent of the energy, and every tonne of paper recycled saves almost 13 trees, 4100 kilowatts of electricity and more than 30,000 litres of water. Yet most people admit to being confused about what they can and can't recycle. Throwing the wrong rubbish in the recycling bin can contaminate the collection and undermine the viability of recycling efforts. Go to www.recyclingnearyou.com.au to learn more about what your local council recycles.

- Lower waste
- Lower carbon emissions

# think of the baby

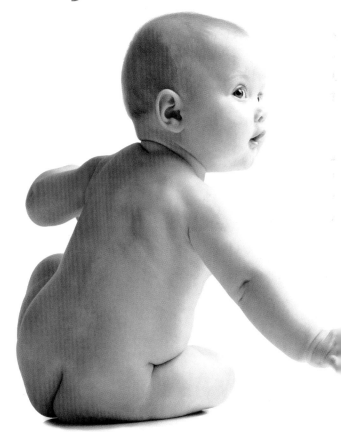

The average baby will have 5500 nappy changes over 2.5 years. More than 800 million disposable nappies are used in Australia every year, requiring the felling of a million trees and 145,000 cubic metres of landfill space. But environmental and consumer agencies rate reuseable cloth nappies as being just as harmful to the environment, depending on what detergent you use and at what temperature you wash them. While disposable nappies create greenhouse gases during the manufacturing process and contribute more to landfill, reusable cloth nappies require large amounts of water, energy and detergents in their washing and drying. Minimise the impact by washing in bulk and choosing disposable brands that are biodegradable and chemical-free.

- Less pollution
- Lower carbon emissions

# power shower

Long showers literally pour resources down the drain, with every minute lingering under the standard showerhead using 15 to 25 litres of water. If you're spending more than five minutes in the shower you're dawdling. If it's more like 10 minutes, over the course of a year you could be wasting enough water to fill a backyard pool and creating an extra tonne of carbon dioxide emissions. Reduce your average shower time from 10 minutes to five and save more than 16,000 litres of water, $90 on the water bill and $150 on water heating. Save even more by setting the thermostat of your water heater to a temperature that doesn't require adding cold water.

- Lower water consumption
- Lower carbon emissions
- Lower water and energy bills

Image © APL

# stem the flow

A third of the water used inside the average home is on showers, while water heating creates a quarter of greenhouse gas emissions from home energy use. Innovative tap and shower fittings can cut the flow by more than half. Compared with a standard showerhead, which might use 15 to 25 litres of water a minute, a water-efficient showerhead can use as little as six or seven litres. Over a year of five-minute showers a single showerhead can save 15,000 litres of water as well as the energy needed to heat that water, saving about $50 per person on water bills and up to $100 per person on power. Look for AAA-rated fittings under the current National Water Conservation Labelling Scheme, and for the new star rating being introduced.

- Lower water consumption
- Lower carbon emissions
- Lower water and energy bills

Image courtesy of Interbath-Australia

# don't flush it all away

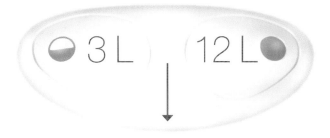

Only 3 per cent of the world's water is fresh, and only a third of that is available for human consumption. In a continent as dry as Australia we can't afford to flush it down the toilet. Yet that is where a quarter of daily household water use – about 170 litres a day – now goes. An old-style single-flush toilet can use up to 12 litres of water in one flush; more modern dual-flush systems average less than four litres. A water-efficient dual-flush toilet can reduce household water use by about 1,000 litres a year. If you have an old toilet, reduce its capacity by filling one or more soft-drink bottles with water and placing them in the cistern.

• Lower water consumption
• Lower water bills

# life's a dish

You may pride yourself on a clean kitchen but the dirty little secret is that the sink – and the dishwasher – accounts for a fifth of average household water use and a tenth of its greenhouse gas emissions from electric water heating. An average automatic dishwasher can use more than 40 litres of water per cycle; an efficient model uses half that. Doing the dishes the old-fashioned way can use even less, depending on your method. A running tap wastes more than 10 litres of water a minute, so wash items together rather than rinsing them individually. Reduce water flow by half without reducing water pressure by installing inexpensive aerators or flow valves in your taps.

- Lower water consumption
- Lower greenhouse emissions
- Lower water and electricity bills

# solar flair

Water heating accounts for a quarter of greenhouse gas produced by an average household's energy use. Every 13 litres of hot water heated by a conventional electric water heater generates about a kilogram of emissions. A much more efficient option is to use the sun's rays to heat your water. With a gas booster kicking in on sunless days, a solar hot water heater should provide most of a household's hot water needs and pay for itself within five years. Locate your booster near the bathroom to minimise heat and water loss. Government rebates are provided for solar heaters, so check with your state authority.

- Lower water consumption
- Lower greenhouse emissions
- Lower water and electricity bills

# photo-opportunity

## 10

Apart from heating water, solar energy can be harnessed through photovoltaic panels that turn light into electricity. In the past using solar panels to generate energy has not been an economical option for most households. But as the technology improves and production costs come down, solar panels are becoming more viable for the average household. Though it is initially expensive to set up, a photovoltaic system will generate power for 30 years and pay for itself after about eight. Soon solar panels will be cheap and effective enough to pay for themselves within two years. There are also generous rebates offered by state and federal governments.

• Lower carbon emissions
• Lower energy bills

Image © APL

# 11 get cosy

Home heating and cooling is responsible for 11 per cent of household greenhouse gas emissions. As much as 35 per cent of heat loss from a house is through an uninsulated ceiling, with a further 15 to 25 per cent through the walls and 10 to 20 per cent through the floor. Insulation material made from jute, glass wool or recycled paper can keep a home cosy and comfortable all year round, minimising the need for heaters in winter and air-conditioners in summer.

- Lower carbon emissions
- Lower energy bills

# seal the cracks

Every degree of difference in the temperature between inside and outside can add up to 10 per cent to the cost of heating or cooling the average home. Make the most of the energy you use by trapping the air rather than having it escape through cracks under doors, between windows and around floor vents. You can cut greenhouse emissions by hundreds of kilograms a year by using inexpensive seals to plug cracks and gaps, fitting dampeners to fireplaces and blocking unnecessary vents.

- Lower carbon emissions
- Lower energy bills

# 13

# join the fan club

Energy demand peaks on hot days as millions of businesses and homes across Australia turn on their air-conditioners. With houses often built for size and view, good passive solar design and orientation is often ignored – and the result is a heat trap. A well-designed home should need nothing more energy-intensive than a ceiling sweep fan (which will also improve an air-conditioner's efficiency). Keep windows and curtains closed during the day to block out the heat, then open them at night to let the house cool. If you must use an air-conditioner, set its thermostat to a balmy 27 degrees rather than an autumnal 24 degrees to reduce the energy used by nearly a third.

- Lower carbon emissions
- Lower energy bills

## 14
# make the most of the day

B anish your daily interior gloom with a natural light source that lets you leave the lights off till the sun goes down. A new generation of highly reflective tubular skylights can bring energy-efficient lighting through tall roofs to rooms deep within two-storey and period homes. The same qualities of reflection can be used to light your home in other ways. Walls painted light colours don't absorb as much light as dark-coloured walls. For down lights, use lower-watt lamps with reflector backs.

• Lower carbon emissions
• Lower energy bills

# have a 15
# light touch

Lighting the average Australian home generates about two-thirds of a tonne of greenhouse gas and costs about $90 a year. Often the lighting is unnecessary – and it is a myth that turning lights on and off uses more electricity than leaving them on. Turn them off if you're out of the room for more than a minute. If you find it hard to remember to do this, relatively inexpensive timer controls and daylight or movement sensors can be installed to switch off lights automatically. Dimmers and lamps also help to reduce unnecessary light use.

- Lower carbon emissions
- Lower energy bills

# use bright ideas

The ordinary incandescent light bulb remains the most popular form of home lighting because it is so cheap. But it is also very inefficient, with most of the electric current that passes through its filament being converted into heat, not light. A 20-watt compact fluorescent light (CFL) provides as much light as a 100-watt incandescent bulb, and lasts about eight times longer. Though a CFL will cost 10 times more to buy than a $1 incandescent globe, over its average life of about five years it will save $80 in electricity and 650 kilograms in greenhouse gas. A lighting shop can generally advise on the best product for your needs, with a better quality CFL lasting up to five times longer than a cheapie.

- Lower carbon emissions
- Lower energy bills

# blow off the heater

Radiators chew energy like there's no climate-friendly tomorrow, with a single electric bar generating about a kilogram of greenhouse gas every hour. Fan heaters are no better; because they rely on convection heating – directly warming air, which then often escapes through doors, windows and vents – they are extremely inefficient at heating a large room. Use them a to heat people, not spaces. Natural gas and reverse-cycle air-conditioners are better alternatives, generating only a third of the emissions of electric radiators and fan heaters. Better still, invite some friends over: every person in your house generates the same amount of warmth as a 100-watt heater.

- Lower carbon emissions
- Lower energy bills

# warm yourself, not the environment

## 18

One of the earliest – and still most efficient – forms of insulation invented was clothing. Long before they became a fashion statement, clothes were helping people survive in a world where there was no artificial air-conditioning to keep the temperature at a shopping-mall-constant 24 degrees. Snuggle up in a jumper or thick socks when you feel winter's chill. If you are still cold, try jumping up and down for a minute. Temperature variations are a natural part of life, and a fit and healthy body should be comfortable enough without excessive artificial heating or cooling. Every one degree you avoid in external heating costs will cut about 3 per cent from your heating bill.

- Lower carbon emissions
- Lower energy bills
- Better health

# 19

# step up to the line

Every load of wet clothes put into an electric clothes dryer generates more than 3 kilograms of greenhouse gas from the energy used. A solar clothes dryer, better known as a clothes line, generates none. Choose the natural solution whenever you can. If it rains while clothes are hanging, consider it a softening rinse. For those times when you must use a dryer, make sure your washing machine's spin cycle removes as much excess water as possible, and keep the dryer's lint filter clean so it operates at maximum efficiency.

- Lower carbon emissions
- Lower energy bills

# it doesn't wash

An average washing machine produces about 90 kilograms of greenhouse gas emissions in a year, but it's when you choose hot water that cleaning clothes gets really dirty. A hot wash generates five times more in greenhouse gas than a cold wash, so choose the cold cycle to save 3 kilograms in emissions per wash. There's no need to throw in more washing detergent to compensate either: the scrubbing action of the washing machine – with front-loading models usually being the most efficient – does most of the work. Every 100 grams of detergent generates 1.3 kilograms of greenhouse gas in their manufacturing process, so use only what is needed. Avoid washing and ironing clothes – jeans, for instance – unnecessarily.

• Lower carbon emissions
• Lower energy bills

# cool it with the fridge

A third of Australian homes have at least two refrigerators. Unless you live in a remote area and need to feed a family the size of the Brady Bunch, this may be a luxury the earth can't afford. Larger or older model fridges can use up to $200 in electricity a year, generating more than 1.5 tonnes of greenhouse gases. Maximise your fridge's efficiency by making sure the seals work and position it in a cool spot. Freezers should be set at 15 to 18 degrees below zero, fresh food compartments at about four degrees – every one degree lower increases energy consumption by up to 5 per cent. When buying a new fridge or freezer, choose one with a high energy star rating.

- Lower carbon emissions
- Lower energy bills

# don't cook up a storm

Cooking in the average Australian home uses enough energy to generate about half a tonne of greenhouse gases a year. It's as simple as making a cup of tea: every 10 litres of water boiled in an electric kettle produces a kilogram of emissions. Minimise energy by cooking efficiently: reuse hot water, put lids on pots, have dishes simmer rather than boil and don't worry about preheating the oven. There is no standard energy rating for cooking appliances but bear in mind that a conventional oven will produce a third more greenhouse emissions than a fan-forced one, an electric stove produces double the emissions of gas or a microwave oven, and bigger appliances are less efficient than smaller ones.

- Lower carbon emissions
- Lower energy bills

# get drastic on plastics

The age of plastic walks hand in hand with the age of oil. Our homes are full of objects made from petrochemicals such as polyethylene, polystyrene, polyvinyl chloride, polypropylene, nylon and acrylic. Yet the properties that make plastic so handy – durability and resistance to degradation – also make it difficult to dispose of. Choose furnishings and household items that will last and can be recycled. Opt for alternatives to plastic made from paper, calico or wood. Use natural plant-based finishes on wood.

- Less pollution
- Healthier home

# soft furnishings

Look for natural furnishings that have been or can be recycled – tables made from reclaimed timber, organic cotton curtains, an organic wool duvet, beeswax candles, bamboo, hemp bedding or jute flooring. Save resources used in the manufacturing of new materials by buying second-hand furniture – old timber products are much more durable than new furniture made from veneer-covered particle board. Or buy new furniture made from recycled materials such as recovered railway sleepers, old phones, computer casings and vacuum cleaners.

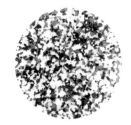

- Lower consumption
- Lower carbon emissions
- Less waste

Furniture made with Recopol™ recycled resin shells.
Images courtesy of Wharington International

# detox your home

The average home contains more chemicals than an early 20th century chemistry laboratory: aerosol cans, paints, furniture polish, glues, ammonia-based cleaners, nail polish remover, oils and battery acid. While the effect of the traces of up to 300 synthetic chemicals that have been found in human bodies is still unclear, for the environment these household chemicals are a proven toxic cocktail when disposed of in landfill or poured down the drain. Check with your local council about its collection days for chemical nasties. Local tips usually accept oil, paints, paint thinners and cleaners, as do some hardware stores.

- Less pollution
- Healthier home

# in the can

Conventional paints use fossil fuels as their basic ingredient, producing greenhouse gases, toxic waste and air pollutants known as volatile organic compounds. Organic and toxin-free brands are not only better for the environment but can also benefit allergy and asthma sufferers, pregnant women and young children. A number of brands offset emissions associated with their production, use and disposal through Greenhouse Friendly accredited abatement projects. Natural wood oils will also prolong the life of timber floors, decks and furniture because, unlike normal polyurethane varnishes, there is no need to sand back the wood before applying.

- Lower carbon emissions
- Less pollution
- Healthier home

Image © APL

# go with the grain

Wood is a perfect renewable and sustainable resource, providing it isn't being clear-felled. Up to 90 per cent of timber from Papua New Guinea and 70 per cent from Indonesia is destructively or illegally logged. Unethically logged wood is used in countries such as China to make furniture for export. To ensure the wood you are buying has come from a forest managed according to internationally agreed social and environmental standards, look for the Forest Stewardship Certified Timber label. This trademark is accredited by the Forest Stewardship Council and endorsed by organisations including the World Wide Fund for Nature, Friends of the Earth and Greenpeace.

- Save old-growth forests
- Reduce greenhouse effect
- Support sustainable industry

# build, don't destroy

## 28

A piece of timber from a local, sustainable plantation has less environmental impact than imported forest timber. Recycled timber has even less impact again. Recycled materials can also save you money and add personality to your environment. You can find bricks, windows, roof tiles, doors, floorings, windows, doors, fireplaces and fittings at salvage and demolition yards. Even when recycled materials are not cheaper, you will be adding value to your home and helping to create a market for recycled resources, which in turn will encourage others to recycle. Look for local materials to save money and energy on transportation.

- Reduce waste
- Save money

# curtain call

## 29

Cut heat transferral through windows by a further third by installing heavy lined drapes with pelmets. Wooden frames provide better insulation than aluminium. Shade east- and west-facing windows with external devices such as blinds or shutters. Cover north-facing windows with suitably angled eaves or pergolas that provide shade during summer and light during winter. Choose glass appropriate to orientation and climate. The Window Energy Rating Scheme will help you select the most energy-efficient option according to heating and cooling performance. Most Australians live in climates where glass technology can help save energy throughout the year, regardless of which direction they face.

- Lower carbon emissions
- Lower energy bills

# get that glazed look

Windows are the weakest link in a well-insulated home, with a square metre of conventional single-glazed glass exposed to direct sun on a hot day generating as much heat as a single-bar radiator. On a cold day that glass will lose up to 10 times more heat than the same area of insulated wall. Double-glazed windows, using two sheets of glass with air sealed between them, are up to twice as expensive but also up to twice as efficient. Use an outer pane that will block unwanted solar radiation and an inner pane that will reduce heat loss from inside.

- Lower carbon emissions
- Lower energy bills

# sleep disorder

That comforting little red or green light emitted expectantly by your television, DVD player, stereo system or computer comes at a price. Every year it is adding about $100 to your electricity bill and creating up to 85 kilograms in unnecessary greenhouse gases. Even in standby or 'sleep' mode, appliances can still be operating at up to 40 per cent of their full running power. Standby power, which often serves no real function (apart from running a clock), accounts for about 10 per cent of Australian household electricity use. Rather than leaving your TV or stereo to chew power for the 80 per cent of time it isn't being used, switch it off at the power point. Buy a power board with individual switches to manage several appliances.

- Lower carbon emissions
- Lower energy bills

# 32
# switch to renewables

Our energy needs will continue to draw on emission-producing non-renewable sources such as coal for as long as we care only about what energy source is cheapest to burn. Increasing numbers of Australians are taking their responsibility to future generations seriously by signing up for renewable power to ensure their energy consumption is not contributing to greenhouse gas emission. Under the government-accredited Green Power scheme your energy provider will source the equivalent of some or all of your energy consumption from renewable sources, such as solar, wind and hydro. It does cost more but your money is used to support crucial investment in renewable energy.

- Lower carbon emissions
- Invest in renewable energy

A quarter of average household water use goes on the garden; more than 90 per cent of that is poured on the lawn.

# in the garden

# go native

Native animals depend on the plants they have evolved with for food and shelter. Though a few hardy species, like possums, have adapted to human transformation of their traditional habitat, most native animals find little attraction in imported lawns and rose gardens. Foreign plants will also guzzle water: running a sprinkler for an hour consumes 1000 litres of water; a standard garden hose uses even more. Native plants will not only attract birds and butterflies but save the time and expense of daily watering. Australia is a continent of enormous biodiversity, so check with your local council, nursery or gardening group about what plants are indigenous to your area.

• Greater biodiversity
• Lower water consumption
• Lower water bills

Photograph Irene Selvage

# multi-storey living

Nature finds its balance in a complex network of mutual dependence, with each species providing several useful benefits to other flora and fauna. A tree might feed one animal and shelter another. In natural bushland there are five main layers of vegetation in which different animals live. Try to replicate this in your garden with a combination of tall trees (eucalypts, for instance), smaller trees and tall shrubs (banksias, bottlebrushes, tea trees and wattles), shrubs (correas, hakeas), groundcover (grasses and creepers) and a litter layer of leaf matter, fallen branches, logs and rocks. Use terracotta pipes as substitutes for hollow logs to give small marsupials and lizards a place to hide from predators such as cats and dogs.

- Greater biodiversity
- Lower water consumption
- Lower water bills

Image © APL

# 35
# cover up

Up to 90 per cent of all the water used on Australian gardens, or about a quarter of total household water consumption, goes on lawns. Consider replacing little-used grass areas, such as your front yard, with a native garden that reduces street noise, increases privacy and can save you the cost of a fence. Groundcover can thrive where grass does poorly. Putting mulch around your plants and on lawn can cut the amount of water lost through evaporation by up to 70 per cent. It also limits weed growth and can improve soil conditions. Pine bark mulch can even be used for children's play areas: it is just as safe as grass and requires no watering.

• Lower water consumption
• Lower water bills

# shady characters

Plants not only lower greenhouse emissions and provide habitats for wildlife; they can also lower home energy costs. Trees with high canopies on the west side of your property will provide shade from the afternoon sun. Shrubs that allow filtered light and breezes are appropriate for more localised shading of east- and west-facing windows. Deciduous trees and vines, even though not indigenous, are useful on your home's northern side, providing foliage to shade against the summer sun while allowing light and warmth during winter. Even small plants will help cool your home, through the evaporative process called transpiration.

- Lower energy consumption
- Lower energy bills

# liquid asset

Imagine watering the garden every time you have a shower or filling the toilet cistern whenever you wash your hands. Only about half of the water used by the average household needs to be of crystal-clear drinking quality. Water for the toilet and the garden can be recycled from basins, showers, washing machines and the kitchen sink using so-called grey water recycling systems. The higher content of chemicals like phosphorus and nitrogen in grey water can even be a source of nutrients for plants. A grey water system can be anything from a tank collecting laundry water to a comprehensive system using plants and micro-organisms to treat water from all household outlets. Check with your local council and water authority about rebates for approved systems.

- Lower demand on water supply
- Lower water bills

# 38

# think tank

While dam levels fall, the vast majority of the rain run-off in urban areas is channelled along gutters and down pipes straight into the drain. The rain that falls on your roof can be collected in a tank and used on the garden, to fill the pool, for flushing toilets, doing the laundry, showering or even drinking. Every 100 millimetres of rainfall running off the average home roof can provide enough water for several weeks of total household consumption. You can get rebates for installing a rainwater tank, so check with your water authority or local council.

• Lower demand on water supply
• Lower water bills

# live under a flight path

Birds bring life to a garden, providing colour, movement, sound and useful fertilisation and pest-control services. With just 6 per cent of the Australian landmass reserved for national parks, the urban garden is a valuable potential habitat. Make your garden a desirable destination for lorikeets, galahs, honeyeaters and rosellas. Birds like taller trees for roosting and nesting, shrubs for flowers and fruits, and clearings to hunt for seeds and insects. Hollow logs or bird boxes as well as a fresh water supply will put more feathers in your cap. So will keeping your garden predator-free; if you must have a cat, put a bell on its collar and try to keep it inside.

- Greater biodiversity
- Lower insect population
- Easier gardening

Photograph Irene Selvage

# make a clean sweep

The new status symbol of the urban gardener is the eco-efficient broom or rake. Until someone invents concrete that grows, hosing the leaves off the driveway and footpath is out. So is powering up a two-stroke petrol engine to give the lawn a quick blow. Leaf blowers or air brooms are not only a source of noise pollution for the neighbours on Sunday mornings but can produce the same amount of air pollutants in an hour as driving a car from Brisbane to Sydney. Eliminating all petrol-powered mowers, blowers, snippers and trimmers would cut as much air pollution as taking a quarter of the nation's vehicles off the road.

- Lower carbon emissions
- Lower noise
- More exercise

Image © APL

# grow your own
# fruit and veggies

41

Even unprocessed foods contain 'embodied energy' – the fuel and water consumed in growing, harvesting, transporting, storing and selling. The further your food travels to reach your plate, the greater the energy and associated greenhouse emissions. Having your own fruit and vegetable patch is therefore not only a source of guaranteed fresh organic produce but also very eco-efficient. A kitchen garden can also be a source of fresh herbs for daily cooking, as well as personally satisfying and a great motivation to get outside and do some incidental exercise.

• Lower carbon emissions
• Better eating
• Lower grocery bills

# natural born killers

Nature regulates itself. A garden dependent on artificial fertilisers and pesticides is flawed in design. Fertilisers, synthesised from fossil fuels or dug up from Pacific islands, can harm native wildlife by promoting the growth of weeds that compete for resources. When washed into waterways they encourage algal growth, killing fish. Pesticides, meanwhile, kill beneficial insects along with pests, can directly harm other species and pose a threat to humans when they accumulate in the food chain. Choose eco-efficient gardening solutions. Native plants will thrive without fertiliser. Insect-eating animals and complementary planting of natural herbicides will reduce the need for pesticides. Use an organic pesticide made out of capsicum, garlic or chilli to control aphids and caterpillars.

- Lower carbon emissions
- Healthier environment
- Less time and money spent on garden

# 43

# get to the roots

Watering systems that deliver water as closely to plant roots as possible can reduce evaporation losses by up to 75 per cent. The most efficient and low-maintenance watering system is sub-surface drip irrigation, using pipes with small perforations below the soil surface to deliver droplets at a rate of two, four or eight litres an hour. A simple sub-surface watering device can be made by cutting the top off a plastic bottle and punching holes in its base. Bury the bottle about 20 to 30 centimetres from the base of the target plant, deep enough so it will release water about 10 centimetres below the surface of the soil.

- Less water use
- Lower water bills

# from dusk to dawn

Image © APL

P lants and soil lose water during the day through evaporation. Watering during the cooler times of the day gives the water a chance to percolate through the soil and be absorbed by the roots of the plants. In hot conditions it is better to water in the evening. In cooler conditions, though, plants can develop fungal growth from water on their leaves overnight, so it is preferable to water early in the morning. Group thirsty plants together and water them longer but less often to encourage deeper roots and increase their drought tolerance.

- Less water consumption
- Lower water bills

# back to the earth

Food scraps and garden clippings make up about 40 per cent of household waste. When this organic matter ends up in landfill and decomposes without air it produces methane, a greenhouse gas 20 times more potent than carbon dioxide. A compost heap or worm farm is a simple but effective way to cleanly convert waste from the kitchen or garden into something productive. Each tonne of organic matter you divert from the rubbish bin will prevent the creation of a third of a tonne of greenhouse gases in landfill. Compost is also the perfect natural fertiliser, containing all the necessary elements to improve soil structure, microbial activity and water containment.

- Less waste
- Save money on gardening bills

# use the landscape

Make a feature of the contours in your garden by landscaping for water efficiency. Make the most of water running off sloping, rocky and paved areas by bordering them with plant beds to absorb the water. Create depressions or ponds where water can collect to seep back into the ground and replenish the water table rather than going straight down the storm-water drain. A permanent pond is a valuable addition to a garden ecosystem, attracting birds and frogs. With the right plantings it will provide a habitat for native fish, which in turn will eat mosquitoes, other insects and algae.

- Less water waste
- Healthier garden
- Healthier environment

# 47
# pave the way

Roofs, roads, driveways, footpaths and other water-resistant surfaces stop rainfall being absorbed into the ground to be used by plants and filtered by the soil before entering the water table. The run-off instead flows untreated down drains and is dumped directly into waterways, flooding the ecosystem with chemicals and other pollutants. The amount of water lost down the stormwater drain is many times that used in the average garden. Lessen the loss by minimising paved areas and using permeable pavers or paving designs that provide gaps for the rainwater to reach the earth.

- Less water waste
- Healthier garden
- Healthier environment

# in the swim

A pool can lose its equivalent volume in water every year as a result of evaporation and over-cleaning. Ensure your pool is not a huge water drain by filling it from rainwater catchment. Install a backwash storage system where the water is stored to let chlorine dissipate and then discharged into a vegetated area of the garden rather than into the stormwater system. Cover your pool when it is not in use to minimise evaporation; this will also help keep it clean, saving on chemical cleaners. Minimise the need for chlorine, which can be harmful to the environment and human health, by using an alternative cleaning system such as an ionising water purifier. Ask your pool supplier about the options.

- Lower water use
- Healthier environment
- Lower water and cleaning bills

Paper comprises up to 70 per cent of office waste, with 10,000 A4 sheets used for every Australian worker each year. That's equal to 10 million trees.

at work

# lunch is on you

Buying your lunch is arguably more water and energy-efficient than making it yourself, but a home-packed lunch is undoubtedly cheaper and produces less solid waste than fast food. Food courts and other public places can be neglectful in providing recycling bins, with glass bottles, paper napkins, polystyrene plates, plastic cutlery and food scraps all going into the one bin for disposal in landfill. Save resources and money by bringing your lunch in a reusable container. Rather than buying new plastic containers, reuse takeaway containers before throwing them into the recycling bin. Reuse bread wrappers and other plastic packaging rather than buying plastic film or aluminium foil.

• Less waste
• Save money

# it's a mug's game

Coffee has become an indispensable part of the working day, but why not dispense with disposable cups? Life cycle analysis of the energy and waste from producing, transporting and disposing of cardboard or polystyrene cups shows the mug to be far more eco-efficient – even taking into account the water needed to wash it between uses. Over its life a mug will be used about 3000 times, resulting in 30 times less solid waste and 60 times less air pollution than using the equivalent number of cardboard cups. Most takeaway coffee joints will be happy to make your favourite brew in your own favourite mug – after all, it saves their business money – and you are likely to get a slightly larger coffee fix for your effort.

- **Less energy use**
- **Lower carbon emissions**
- **Less waste**

Image © APL

# stay in the black

## 51

Dire warnings against reusing printer ink and toner cartridges help protect the profit margins of manufacturers but also contribute to more than 1,500 tonnes of environmentally unfriendly cartridges ending up in Australian landfill each year. Subject to the fine print on a warranty, however, there is no reason why a cartridge can't be reused up to four times. You will cut waste and save up to 90 per cent on the cost of a new cartridge. Use a refiller or remanufacturer prepared to offer a written guarantee against equipment damage and downtime caused by using their products.

• Less waste
• Save money

re-fill

# turn over an old leaf

Despite advances in technology, the paperless office remains a futuristic fantasy, with about 10,000 sheets of A4 paper – as much paper as is produced from pulping a full-grown tree – being used by every Australian worker each year. Much of this paper comes from native eucalypt forests and is chlorine-bleached, a process that produces toxic dioxins. The simplest way to cut down paper use is to use both sides. Set the printer and photocopier defaults so that you have to choose *not* to print double-sided. Minimise the potential for wastage through paper jams by storing paper in a dry spot and loading it into the copier the right way up (it actually does make a difference).

- Conserve forests
- Less waste
- Save money

# 53

# treat it like it grows on trees

Paper comprises up to 70 per cent of office waste, so simple recycling measures can significantly reduce an organisation's waste removal expenses. Print out only what is necessary, and proofread documents carefully on screen to avoid having to print multiple copies. Place a tray on your desk to collect single-side printed scrap paper and use it for taking notes or in the photocopier or fax machine. Have a paper-recycling box under your desk and encourage your colleagues to make the effort to walk those extra metres to put their paper in the recycling bin.

- Conserve forests
- Reduce waste
- Save money

Image courtesy of the Australian Greenhouse Office, Department of the Environment and Heritage

# close the loop

A business is not truly recycling unless it buys recycled products. Recycled paper uses up to 90 per cent less water and half the energy required to make paper from virgin timber, yet less than 5 per cent of the 1.2 million tonnes of printing and writing paper used in Australia each year is recycled content. The rest comes from chopping down 30 million trees. While recycled papers were once avoided because they looked inferior, could cause copiers to jam and were unsuitable for archival purposes, it is now often hard to spot the difference, with manufacturers guaranteeing recycled paper for virtually all office functions.

- Conserve forests
- Lower carbon emissions
- Lower energy and water use

Image © APL

# 55

## would the last one out ...

The lights in many offices burn long after workers have ceased to burn the midnight oil. It might make for a pretty skyline but leaving the lights on, combined with all those computers left on standby, can double a company's energy bill. Unnecessary lights also generate unnecessary heat, requiring the air-conditioner to work overtime, using even more electricity. The Australian Greenhouse Office estimates greenhouse gas emissions created by commercial building lighting could be reduced by as much as 70 per cent. Ask your building manager to turn lights off at night or to install movement-activated sensors. Take the initiative by placing reminders near light switches in the area you work.

- Lower carbon emissions
- Save on energy bills

PLEASE TURN THE LIGHTS OFF!

# collect call

Y ou only use your mobile phone recharger for a few hours a week but leaving it plugged into the power point means it could be drawing electricity all the time. The same goes for rechargers of other electronic devices, like laptop computers, PDAs, MP3 players and digital cameras. Unplug them when you're not using them. Phones contain toxic metals – including arsenic, antimony, beryllium, cadmium, copper, lead, nickel and zinc – that do not degrade in the environment, so it is important to recycle them. Mobile Muster is the official industry recycling program, while the Aussie Recycling Program is run in conjunction with state cerebral palsy and spastic societies. Old phones that still work can be exported to developing countries where they can help bridge the digital divide, or be dismantled for parts and their materials recovered to make other products.

- Lower carbon emissions
- Save on energy bills

# start a branch office

The air in your office might be air-conditioned but it is far from clean, with many office products emitting potentially harmful toxins. The air inside a sealed energy-efficient building can be 10 times more polluted than outside, with the CSIRO estimating that the impact on worker health costs the Australian economy $12 billion a year. Indoor plants are natural air filters, absorbing airborne pollutants and radiation from computers while replenishing oxygen levels. Research has found that indoor plants can reduce fatigue, coughs, sore throats and other cold-related illnesses by up to 30 per cent, cutting down on absenteeism. Plants also have a measurable effect on stress levels, helping to keep employees happy and relaxed in the work environment.

• Lower air pollution
• Healthier workplace
• Save on energy bills

# log off and shut down

Many office computers never get switched off, needlessly consuming energy overnight and on weekends. A computer left on all day, every day uses nearly 1,000 kilowatts of electricity over a year, producing more than a tonne of carbon emissions and costing $125. A computer that is switched off at the end of the day uses less than 250 kilowatts, at a cost of $30 per year. Turn off equipment when you go to a meeting or take a break. If you are away from your computer for less than half an hour, put it in sleep mode, which reduces energy use to about 5 per cent of full operating power.

• Lower carbon emissions
• Save on energy bills

# 59
# loosen your collar

Business attire – particularly the traditional businessman's uniform of long-sleeved shirt, tie and jacket – is ill-suited to the Australian climate. During the summer this hot clothing means air-conditioners have to be cranked up to maintain comfortable conditions in offices as well as shops and restaurants, using large amounts of energy and contributing to the greenhouse effect. More climate-appropriate work wear – short-sleeved open-necked shirts, for instance – means your office air-conditioning won't need to be set to such a low temperature. Every degree higher the thermostat is set will cut up to 20 per cent from air-conditioning costs.

- Lower carbon emissions
- Save on energy bills

Image © APL

# taken to the cleaners

You think you're picking up fresh, clean work clothes from the dry-cleaners but you might also be getting a sniff of the industry's dirty environmental laundry. Dry-cleaners use large amounts of the chemical solvent tetrachloroethylene, a powerful degreasing agent that is also a suspected carcinogen, can aggravate asthma and allergies and is harmful to the environment. During its production, transport and use, tetrachloroethylene breaks down into other chemicals – such as the toxin phosgene – and contributes to photochemical smog. Before opting for dry-cleaning, consider the merit of a quick cold hand wash or spot-cleaning. Look for a cleaning service with 'clean and green' processes, including reuse of hangers and garment bags.

- Less pollution
- Healthier environment

# event horizon

Think green next time you are arranging for the printing of business cards, buying office equipment or even booking a conference venue. Consider impacts such as greenhouse gas emissions from travel, energy use, water conservation and waste-minimisation policies. The Green Star rating for commercial buildings is a comprehensive indicator of a building's eco-efficiency. But don't just stop there: ask suppliers about their environmental practices and choose businesses that use and provide recycled goods. The purchasing power of a business can help create more demand for recycling and help bring down the cost of recycled goods.

- Lower carbon emissions
- Lower water use
- Less waste

# a super choice

Most Australians have no idea where or how their superannuation is invested, but new laws promoting choice in super give you a chance to put your money where your mouth is. You now have the option to invest your money according to environmentally and socially responsible criteria. Those criteria might preclude investing in companies in problem sectors like gambling, tobacco and arms production, or preference investment in companies with leading environmental credentials (like renewable power). Ethical funds offer returns that match or outperform general funds. Choose an ethical investment option from an industry super fund, a master fund or a specialist ethical fund manager.

- Support sustainable industry
- Reap higher returns

# call in the auditors

Ask your senior management to commission an environmental audit of your business and the building you work in. A trained environmental consultant will assess the amount of energy, water, waste and materials your company uses, where it is generated and where it goes. An environmental audit can highlight areas of inefficiency and excessive waste, and provide solutions that reduce resource consumption and save money. It is also an effective risk-management tool, helping a business avoid the costly consequences of fines or legal challenges for environmental breaches.

- Improve environmental performance
- Improve business efficiency

# go public

More and more Australians are thinking of the environmental and social implications of their purchasing decisions. More than 90 per cent of us say we want businesses to go beyond their historical role of making profits, paying taxes, employing people and obeying the law. Our purchasing power can reward companies doing good things and penalise those doing nothing. Your company benefits from having a comprehensive environmental policy, an environmental officer and public reporting of its goals and achievements. If your company doesn't do any of these things, ask why not and volunteer to help establish a committee to oversee, measure and report on environmental efforts.

- Improve business reputation
- Promote public accountability

Australians throw away more than 3.4 million tonnes of packaging – 165 kilograms for every man, woman and child – each year. Less than half of it is recycled.

# shopping

# 65

# less is more

Every day we are bombarded by thousands of advertisements encouraging us to equate quality of life with consumption. You might think of it as retail therapy but for the environment it is an affliction. Every item you buy contains embodied energy, water and waste in its production, packaging, transport and disposal. Achieving a sustainable lifestyle means buying a bit less of everything. Before any purchase ask yourself if you really need it. In most cases your life won't be any less full and rich without it, and every dollar you save equates to a saving of about 1.6 kilograms of greenhouse gas emissions.

- Lower energy and water use
- Lower carbon emissions
- Less waste
- Save money

Image © APL

# have a lend

66

Next time you are in a newsagency, bookshop or DVD store, ask yourself if you really need to own something you will probably only read or watch once. Join the local library and video rental store, and borrow rather than buy books and DVDs. See if you can borrow items you seldom use – power tools and camping gear, for instance – from family and friends. Services usually have a lower environmental impact than goods of the same value, so indulge in regular trips to the cinema rather than spending thousands of dollars on equipment to replicate the experience in your own home.

- Lower energy and water use
- Lower carbon emissions
- Less waste
- Save money

# buy second-hand

## 67

Apart from food, clothes shopping has the highest environmental impact of all consumer activities, with about 150,000 litres of water used in the production and transport of the new clothes bought by the average Australian household each year. Resist artificially created fashion cycles and step out in your own recycled style. Rather than buying a new pair of jeans that have undergone an industrial process to give them that worn look, just buy a pre-worn pair. The garments you can find in vintage clothing shops are often better than new items and cost a fraction of the price.

• Lower energy and water use
• Lower carbon emissions
• Less waste
• Save money

# lasting glory

RECHARGE

**B**uying the cheapest toaster, washing machine, DVD player, light globe or battery is rarely the most cost-effective option for your wallet or the environment. Such products are usually made with inferior parts that quickly wear out and cannot be replaced – a dubious design practice known as planned obsolescence that ensures continued demand at the cost of valuable resources and unnecessary waste. Cheap designs also usually preclude effective recycling of components. Investing in well-designed, more durable items that can be repaired, upgraded, reused and recycled saves money in the longer term. Rechargeable batteries, for instance, can be recharged hundreds of times with each charge lasting up to twice as long as a disposable battery, making them an economical option for power-hungry devices like digital cameras.

- Lower energy and water use
- Lower carbon emissions
- Less waste
- Save money

# pack it in

## 69

From soft drinks and sugar satchels to cheese singles and shrink-wrapped avocados, the amount of packaging we consume continues to proliferate. Each year the nation throws away more than 3.4 million tonnes of packaging – 165 kilograms for every man, woman and child – and less than half of it is recycled. If you can't find a recycling bin, take your rubbish with you. All plastics marked 1 to 7 are theoretically recyclable, though some councils only recover 1 (polyethylene terephthalate), 2 (high-density polyethylene) and 3 (polyvinyl chloride). Check with your council and avoid packaging bound for landfill. Buy in bulk where you can, and favour fresh produce from local markets over plastic-wrapped supermarket goods. Choose reusable packs – and reuse them.

- Lower energy and water use
- Lower carbon emissions
- Less waste
- Save money

# refuse plastic bags

The Say No to Plastic Bags campaign spearheaded by Clean Up Australia has helped reduce national annual consumption of shopping bags by about 2 billion since 2003. Now Australians go through only 5 billion bags a year. Their use can be measured in minutes – the time it takes you to get from the shop to home – but the bags can last for anything from 20 to 1000 years. Most go into landfill – but an estimated 50 million don't. Let loose in the wild, those bags entangle birds and are swallowed with lethal effect by thousands of whales, turtles and other sea creatures. The oceans are also now full of tiny fragments of plastic working their way into the food chain. Take a reusable bag when you go shopping and say no to plastic bags offered at shops.

- Lower energy and water use
- Lower carbon emissions
- Less waste
- Healthier environment

# balance your diet

About 500 litres of water is required to produce a kilogram of potatoes, 5000 litres to produce a kilogram of rice and anywhere between 50,000 and 100,000 litres to produce a kilogram of beef. Cattle, sheep and other livestock account for more than half of agricultural water use, which in turn accounts for two-thirds of Australia's total water consumption. Agriculture is the second largest source of greenhouse gases after the energy sector, with the methane from flatulent sheep and cattle accounting for 14 per cent of Australia's emissions. Livestock also damage the environment by trampling native vegetation and compacting soil with their hoofs. Choose to eat less resource-intensive meat such as kangaroo and chicken, and eat more grains, fruit and vegetables.

- Lower energy and water use
- Lower carbon emissions

# 72 eat it

W hile wasting resources on excessive food packaging is bad enough, wasting food, which has far greater embodied energy and water, is worse. We eat more than we need – as the nation's expanding waistline attests – and buy more than we eat. Research by the Australia Institute estimates that a quarter of the food purchased – worth some $5.3 billion a year, or about $650 per household – ends up in landfill. The worst offenders are young people and those on high incomes. Take to heart that old advice to eat everything on your plate, make the effort to reuse leftovers, and buy only what you need.

# there's a catch

Seafood has long been considered an aphrodisiac and more recently science has identified the health benefits of fish oil, but rising consumption is putting increased pressure on fish stocks. Since the early 1990s the number of local species threatened by overfishing has risen from five to 18. The Australian Marine Conservation Society, which publishes *Australia's Sustainable Seafood Guide*, recommends avoiding tasty but overfished varieties like orange roughie (often sold as 'sea perch'), eastern gemfish, broadbill swordfish and shark (otherwise known as flake). Better choices include yellowfin bream, blue swimmer crabs, oysters, yabbies and Australian native salmon.

- Save endangered species
- Protect biodiversity

# 74

# edible packaging

F or eco-efficient and fully biodegradable food packaging, choose fresh fruit and vegetables. Their skins are more than adequate protection for transporting them from the shop to your home and can be recycled as compost to feed your garden. Raw fruit and vegetables, as well as legumes and nuts, also use less energy and water than refined and processed food. Eating more raw food is not only cheaper but also healthier, reducing the risk of obesity, allergies, heart disease, cancer and other ailments. So rediscover the pleasure of biting into a crunchy apple rather than a chocolate bar. You'll feel and look better for it.

- Lower energy and water use
- Lower carbon emissions
- Less waste
- Save money

# 75 trade fair

Globalised food production often results in the export of exploitative practices to the third world, with multinational conglomerates dictating prices in markets lacking adequate labour and environmental safeguards. The consequences include abandonment of traditional farming practices, the clearing of rainforests to create more arable land, and the planting of single-variety cash crops dependent on artificial fertilisers and pesticides. By contrast, Fairtrade-branded products are sourced directly from local co-operatives, putting more money in the pockets of growers who can then invest in more sustainable farming as well as their children's education. Look for Fairtrade products, including coffee, tea, cocoa and chocolate at your supermarket, organic food store or Oxfam shop.

- Promote sustainable agriculture
- Reduce inequality
- Healthier eating

Image © APL

# as nature intended

Organic produce, grown without the use of fossil-fuel based fertilisers, synthetic pesticides or genetic modification, is becoming increasingly popular as we become more concerned about the health risks of chemical-laden food. In contrast to non-organic farming, where nutrients are applied to the soil in a soluble form, organic farming focuses on the underlying health of the soil, with plants taking up nutrients released naturally from humus by microbes. The environmental dividend is greater biodiversity at all levels of the food chain. Organic produce has been proven to contain significantly higher concentrations of essential vitamins and minerals. Plus it usually tastes better.

- Lower energy and water use
- Lower carbon emissions
- Healthier environment
- Healthier eating

# 77

## star quality

Energy rating labels are mandatory on fridges, freezers, air-conditioners, washing machines, clothes dryers and dishwashers. The rating is determined by energy efficiency as well as product size, so a bigger appliance with a high rating might still use more energy than a smaller appliance with a lower rating. Many home electronics and office products also carry an energy star label. Some machines, like computers, have energy-saving features that must first be activated, so make sure you do so. Also, look for goods carrying the Good Environmental Choice label, which indicates the environmental performance of a product from a whole-of-product-life perspective.

- Lower carbon emissions
- Lower energy bills

# clean living

The very products and processes used to keep indoor environments clean may also contribute to indoor pollution. Apart from poisoning through ingestion – mostly by small children – studies show that in certain conditions many everyday household cleaners and air fresheners emit toxic contaminants at levels that pose risks to our health. Common symptoms include eye, nose and throat irritation, headaches, dizziness and fatigue. Long-term or cumulative environmental consequences, such as contamination of surface and ground water, may also occur. Clean up with a micro-fibre cleaning cloth, warm water, a dash of natural soap and good old-fashioned elbow grease. Ingredients like vinegar, lemon juice and bicarbonate of soda are effective on tougher stains.

• Healthier environment
• Healthier home

# 79
# get personal

Hair sprays, shaving foams, shampoos, deodorants, fragrances and other personal care products contain a range of active ingredients that are dangerous in high doses. Many cosmetics and toiletries have been found to contain chemicals that are either known carcinogens or are simply untested – of the many thousands of synthetic chemicals used in everyday household items, less than 20 per cent have been tested for acute effects and less than 10 per cent for chronic, reproductive or mutagenic effects. While the small amounts of these ingredients that you absorb through the skin may not be enough to cause any noticeable harm, when washed down the drain they accumulate at levels equal to agrochemicals. Look for natural alternatives.

• Healthier environment
• Healthier home

# moral fibre

While synthetic textiles such as nylon, polyester and lycra are produced from fossil fuels, opting for natural fibres is not the clear-cut environmental choice you might think. Cotton is the world's most chemical-intensive crop, requiring 10 to 18 applications of herbicides, insecticides and fungicides, as well as up to 29,000 litres of water per kilogram produced. Wool, meanwhile, requires a whopping 170,000 litres of water per kilogram and is associated with soil compaction caused by sheep hoofs, pesticide applications to manage lice and flies, habitat loss due to demand for fertiliser-dependant pasture and potent methane emissions. Chemical-free, organic cotton, wool and hemp are the best options.

- Lower water use
- Lower pollution
- Healthier environment

# going the 81 extra mile

D on't let your food be more travelled than you. The average supermarket item is transported hundreds, if not thousands, of kilometres, with the amount of food shipped between nations growing fourfold over the past 40 years as supermarket giants source cheap products from poorer nations with lower labour costs or richer nations that dump subsidised agricultural produce on the international market. But the further the food travels, the greater the associated carbon emissions. Reduce your food miles by buying local produce at the local growers' market. Check labels to see how far the food has come and choose seasonal fruit and vegetables that aren't from half a world away.

- Lower carbon emissions
- Healthier economy

Image © APL

# check the bottom line

It is easy to see the environmental problems caused by heavy industry such as mining and energy production, but the truth is that all companies affect the environment through their business practices and decisions. A bank or insurance company, for instance, can make a difference through policies that give better rates or premiums for more eco-efficient homes or cars. Check the environmental credentials of every business you give money to and compare its efforts with its competitors. If it can't show any environmental commitment – or worse, turns out to be actively lobbying against initiatives like the Kyoto Protocol – then take your business elsewhere.

- Healthier environment
- Greater customer satisfaction

The average Australian car produces about 4.3 tonnes of greenhouse pollution each year. Half the trips we drive are distances short enough to walk or ride.

# travel

# leg it

The average family car travels about 15,000 kilometres a year, generating about 4.3 tonnes of greenhouse pollution and costing more than $2000 in petrol alone. As well as greenhouse pollution, vehicle exhaust contributes to smog, which kills about 4,000 Australians every year – more than the number killed in traffic accidents. Create a healthier environment by getting in some of those 10,000 steps you need to take every day to stay fit. Walk to the local shops rather than taking the car to a distant shopping centre. Go for a hike rather than a drive in the country. Every litre of petrol you avoid using saves 2.3 kilograms in greenhouse pollution.

- Lower carbon emissions
- Lower air pollutants
- Save money
- More exercise

# get on your
## bike

Greenhouse emissions from transport – Australia's third-largest contribution to global warming – are rising faster than any other sector as we adopt lifestyles built around hopping in the car to get to work, collect the groceries, drop the kids off at school, pick up takeaway food and return the videos. Half of all car trips are less than 5 kilometres – a distance research has shown can be covered just as quickly on a bike once traffic and parking is taken into account. Cycling is eco-efficient and fun. Rather than driving to the gym, cycle to work one day a week. A 20-kilometre trip once a week is worth about half a tonne of greenhouse gas emissions over a year.

- Lower carbon emissions
- Lower air pollutants
- Save money
- More exercise

# become a passenger

Cars comprise up to 80 per cent of traffic on Australian roads, with fewer than two in 10 Australians ever using public transport, and fewer than one in 10 regularly using public transport to travel to work or study (and only one in every 20 walking or cycling). Over a year, taking a bus instead of driving a car for a typical 15-kilometre commute saves up to 1.9 tonnes of carbon-dioxide emissions and reduces air pollutants such as carbon monoxide, nitrogen oxide, particulate matter, volatile organic compounds and benzene. Using public transport leads to improved and more efficient services as well as quicker travel times due to lower traffic congestion.

- Lower carbon emissions
- Lower air pollutants
- Save money

# think small

For every 100 kilometres travelled, Australia's vehicle fleet uses an average of 11.3 litres of fuel – the same as in the 1960s. Bigger, heavier cars, particularly so-called sport utility vehicles – many of which never see terrain bumpier than the shopping-centre car park – have offset improvements in fuel efficiency. Driving a large 4WD in city traffic can use up to 25 litres per 100 kilometres, compared with about 15 litres for a traditional six-cylinder family wagon and 12 litres for a smaller four-seater sedan. Compared with a 4WD, driving a smaller call over a typical year's use (15,000 kilometres) will cost $2500 less in petrol and produce four tonnes less carbon dioxide.

• Lower carbon emissions
• Lower air pollutants
• Save money

# emission control

It takes 17 trees to absorb the more than 4 tonnes of carbon dioxide produced by the average car in a year. The non-profit organisation Greenfleet will plant them on your behalf for far less than the cost of just one tank of petrol. For $40 (tax-deductible) you can sign up your car based on average emissions. Or go the extra mile and calculate the greenhouse gases produced by your particular vehicle – the biggest 4WDs will need 30 trees – home/office energy use and air travel. Since 1997, Greenfleet has planted more than 2 million trees – equivalent to taking 117,600 cars off the road. The trees also help tackle dryland salinity, improve water quality and provide habitats for native species.

- Offset total vehicle emissions
- Improve biodiversity

# choose a hybrid

A family-sized hybrid-engine car is more fuel-efficient than even the smallest conventional models. Using both an internal combustion engine and an electric motor, a hybrid car charges electric batteries from both its internal-combustion engine and the kinetic energy dissipated during deceleration. Its electric motor helps to accelerate the car, takes over while cruising or when idling, and otherwise acts as a generator. When the batteries run low, the petrol engine kicks in, recharging them in the process. A hybrid engine uses less than five litres of fuel for each 100 kilometres travelled, and burns fuel more cleanly, with up to half the emissions of a comparable sized car.

- Lower carbon emissions
- Lower air pollutants
- Save money

electric battery + petrol =

save

# soft-pedal

How you drive when you drive can make a big difference to the amount of fuel you consume. By accelerating slowly, driving at moderate speed and avoiding the need for hard braking you can dramatically increase the kilometres you get from a tank of fuel. Avoid high speeds: at 110 km/h your car uses a quarter more fuel than cruising at 90 km/h. A car engine also produces about 40 per cent more emissions when cold, so avoid short trips. Plan your journey to combine multiple errands and, if possible, avoid peak-hour traffic. Keeping your car well-maintained and tyres inflated to the correct level also helps fuel efficiency.

- Lower carbon emissions
- Lower air pollutants
- Save money

REDUCE SPEED NOW

# 90
## small strokes

Three in every four car trips involves transporting a single occupant – the driver. If you aren't taking a passenger, a small scooter or electric bicycle is an obvious choice – particularly as an alternative to a household's second car – when it's too far or inconvenient to walk, cycle or use public transport. A larger scooter with a 250cc engine will use less than four litres of petrol per 100 kilometres, and a 50cc engine as little as 1.5 litres. Scooters are also cheaper and easier to park. With the thousands of dollars you save in running costs and fuel emissions, you could catch a cab when it's raining or rent a car for a weekend away.

- Lower carbon emissions
- Lower air pollutants
- Save money

# fuel around

Not all fuels are equal. High-octane fuel, which contains up to a third less sulphur than regular unleaded petrol, provides more engine power, more efficient consumption and cleaner exhaust emissions. Use a brand with Greenhouse Friendly certification, where the price of the petrol also pays for abatement projects offsetting the carbon emissions produced by the petrol's production and use. Look for petrol blended with biofuels made from renewable or recycled sources, such as ethanol (made from cereals and sugarcane) and biodiesel (derived from vegetable oils or animal waste). A 10 per cent ethanol blend produces a third of the air pollutants of conventional petrol. Buy established brands to be sure it has been correctly blended at the refinery.

- Lower carbon emissions
- Lower air pollution
- Healthier environment

Image courtesy of the Australian Greenhouse Office, Department of the Environment and Heritage

# the sky's the limit

## 92

Probably the single worst thing you can do for the environment is to jet around for business or holidays. Air travel produces about as much carbon dioxide as each passenger driving their own car the same distance – and aircraft emissions, released high in the atmosphere, have a greenhouse effect three times greater than road vehicle emissions. A single return trip to Europe contributes more to global warming than an average Australian's emissions from all other sources over a year. Join a carbon-offset scheme like Carbon Neutral and plan a holiday that's as much about the journey as the destination. Wherever you go be an ecotourist: take nothing but pictures, leave nothing but footprints, kill nothing but time.

- Lower carbon emissions
- Lower air pollution
- Healthier environment

An editor who receives 10 letters on the same issue takes interest; a politician who receives 100 letters takes notice.

# in the community

# 93

# sit down and be counted

An editor who receives 10 letters on the same issue takes interest, a politician who receives 100 takes notice and a chief executive who receives 1000 letters takes action. Decision-makers hear from the public far less than you would expect, so they presume each letter represents the views of dozens, or even hundreds, of people who never got around to writing. And contrary to popular opinion, public servants often crave greater community feedback. Set yourself the task of writing one letter a month, or even a week. Rather than complain, make positive suggestions. Even a single letter published in the local newspaper can be the catalyst for thought and action.

- Change policies
- Change opinions

# sharing is caring

Sharing builds relationships and communities, and reduces your ecological footprint. Share your tools, yours toys and your time – and most importantly your home. The growth in sole households is the single greatest contributor to the growth in household carbon emissions, with people living alone using more energy and resources than those who live with others. A person living alone produces double the waste of someone sharing with three others, and single households also waste resources by duplicating the need for household goods such as washing machines, sofas, microwave ovens, TVs, vacuum cleaners and cooking utensils.

- Lower carbon emissions
- Lower waste
- Lower consumption

# money talks

If you've bought shares in companies directly, consider selling them and reinvesting the money through an ethical investment fund. The increasing financial clout of these funds is an important driver of more sustainable business practices. Their investments provide crucial dollars for research and development, which leads to more efficient use of renewable or recycled resources. Cheaper prices lead to greater demand, which in turn creates economies of scale and even lower production costs. If you've only got a savings account, choose a community-based bank or credit union that provides affordable loans to not-for-profit enterprises like childcare or health services.

- Reward environmental performance
- Expand the market for sustainable products
- Profit without guilt

# support local enterprise

Small local businesses are not only the backbone of the national economy but of vibrant local communities. They create more local jobs, result in more money being reinvested back into the local community and provide more scope for local producers than large chain retailers. Local trade reduces the energy used in transportation. Rather than doing all your grocery shopping in one big hit at the supermarket, spend a little extra time visiting the local grocer, butcher and baker. The experience will be more enjoyable and you'll often find yourself surprised at how much better value the produce is compared with the mass-retailed wares of the industry giants.

• Support the local economy
• Lower transport costs
• Lower carbon emissions and packaging waste

# show co-operative spirit

Co-operatives can be found in many walks of life – from organic growers' markets and friendly societies to housing collectives, credit unions, community radio stations and internet service providers. They pool assets for the shared gain of their members, be they producers, consumers or workers, creating local investment, services and jobs (reducing the need for commuting). Whatever profits they make (if that is their intention) are also more likely to be reinvested in the local community, and on less wasteful consumption (piano lessons rather than a new 6-bedroom holiday home, for instance). Co-operatives can also create products and services that other companies might not regard as profitable enough, building a market for more sustainable business practices.

- Support the local economy
- Encourage sustainable business

# get involved

So often the concentration of media coverage on national or international issues, and the global magnitude of the environmental challenges we face, can leave us feeling powerless and thinking that any action is futile. But the problems we need to tackle are usually very close to home, in our very neighbourhood if not our own homes. There are thousands of local groups making a difference across Australia – planting trees, running op shops, recycling goods, turning used cooking oil into biodiesel or promoting fair trade. If you can't find a group that fits your interests, get together a few like-minded souls and start your own. That's how Clean Up Australia began.

• Improve the local environment
• Offset carbon emissions
• Encourage sustainable business

# let it be a lesson

The thrifty lessons we were taught as children – *waste not, want not*, for instance – turn out to be deep-seated environmental wisdom. The habits we learn early are the usually the ones we keep. Combine your community involvement with a learning experience by supporting (or starting) a sustainability initiative at your local school. It could be a permaculture garden, with the fresh produce being used in the school canteen, a 'walking bus' program to get the children to and from school, an organic food co-operative or a second-hand school uniform and bookstore, or a recycling drive to raise money for the school or a charitable cause.

- Improve the local environment
- Offset carbon emissions
- Encourage a sustainable future

Artwork by Lachlan Chang

# the secret of happiness

## 100

Image © APL

Though many aspects of our culture encourage us to believe the important thing in life is to be rich and famous, extensive academic research across different countries has shown that happiness has little to do with spending money. The most contented people are those who spend their time helping others and contributing to their community. From peeling potatoes in a soup kitchen to working pro bono, volunteering gives you an opportunity not only to increase the social capital of the nation – the cornerstone of its economic prosperity – but also to find personal fulfilment in an activity that doesn't revolve around consuming resources. Reduce. Reuse. Recycle.

- Maker the world a nicer place
- Reduce your environmental footprint
- Be happier and healthier

# websites

| Footprint calculators | Ecological Footprint | www.ecofoot.org |
|---|---|---|
| | Safe Climate Calculator | www.safeclimate.net/calculator |
| | Greenhouse Calculator | www.epa.vic.gov.au/GreenhouseCalculator/calculator/loader.htm |
| | Emissions Calculator | www.elementree.com.au/calculator.asp |
| **Water saving** | Water-saving Tips | www.savewater.com.au |
| | Water Calculators | www.thinkwater.act.gov.au |
| | Waterwise House | www.watercorporation.com.au/savingwater |
| | Interactive House | www.sydneywater.com.au/SavingWater/InteractiveHouse |
| **Energy saving** | Energy Smart | www.energysmart.com.au |
| | Greenhouse Gases | www.greenhousegases.gov.au |
| | Whitegoods Profiler | www.helphouse.com.au/whitegoods.html |
| | Green Power | www.greenpower.gov.au/pages |
| **Home and garden** | Your Home | www.greenhouse.gov.au/yourhome |
| | Building Environment Rating System | www.nabers.com.au |
| | Good Wood Guide | www.greenpeace.org.au/goodwoodguide/index.html |
| | Sustainable Gardening | www.sgaonline.org.au |
| **New homes** | Window Energy Rating Scheme | www.wers.net |
| | BASIX (NSW) | www.basix.nsw.gov.au |
| | 5 Star House (Victoria) | www.5starhouse.vic.gov.au |
| | Energy Smart (WA) | www1.energysmartdirectory.com |
| **Directory services** | Ecospecifier | www.ecospecifier.org |
| | Green Pages | www.greenpagesaustralia.com.au |
| | Green Directory | www.thegreendirectory.com.au |
| | Green Plumbers | www.greenplumbers.com.au |
| **At work** | Eco Office | www.ecooffice.com.au |
| | Eco Purchasing | www.ecobuy.org.au |
| | Greener Print Procurement Guide | www.srd.org.au/gppg.htm |
| | Australian Building Greenhouse Rating | www.abgr.com.au/new/default.asp |
| | Environment Business Australia | www.environmentbusiness.com.au |
| | Corporate Responsibility Index | www.corporate-responsibility.com.au |
| **Environmental labelling** | Energy Rating | www.energyrating.gov.au |
| | Energy Star | www.energystar.gov.au |
| | Greenhouse Friendly | www.greenhouse.gov.au/greenhousefriendly |
| | Good Environmental Choice | www.aela.org.au |
| | Water Conservation Rating | www.wsaa.asn.au/ratings/ratingsabout.htm |

| | | |
|---|---|---|
| Local Recycling | Recycling Near You | www.recyclingnearyou.com.au |
| Computer Recycling | Business to Community Recyclers | www.b2crecyclers.com.au |
| | Australian Computer Society | www.iss.net.au/pc_rec_sig |
| | Dell Recycling (for any brand) | www.dell.com.au/recycle/home |
| | Computer Angels | www.computerangels.org.au |
| Phone Recycling | Mobile Muster | www.mobilemuster.com.au |
| | Mobile Phone Recycling | www.mobilephonerecycling.com.au |
| Investment | Ethical Investment Association | www.eia.org.au |
| | Industry Super Funds | www.industrysuper.com |
| Food | Sustainable Table | www.sustainabletable.org/home |
| | Organic Federation of Australia | www.ofa.org.au |
| | Sustainable Seafood Guide | www.amcs.org.au |
| Shopping | Say No to Plastic Bags | www.noplasticbags.org.au |
| | Australian Co-ops | www.australia.coop |
| | Fair Trade Association | www.fta.org.au |
| | Rechargeable Batteries | www.eneloop.com.au |
| Travel | Green Vehicle Guide | www.greenvehicleguide.gov.au |
| | Greenfleet | www.greenfleet.com.au |
| | Carbon Neutral | www.carbonneutral.com.au |
| | Ecotourism Australia | www.ecotourism.org.au |
| For the kids | Bigfoot | www.powerhousemuseum.com/education/ecologic/bigfoot/mid |
| | Planet Slayer | www.abc.net.au/science/planetslayer |
| Green groups | Australian Conservation Foundation | www.acfonline.org.au |
| | Clean Up Australia | www.cleanup.com.au |
| | Clean Up the World | www.cleanuptheworld.org |
| | Conservation Volunteers Australia | www.conservationvolunteers.com.au |
| | Friends of the Earth | www.foe.org.au |
| | Greenpeace | www.greenpeace.org.au |
| | Keep Australia Beautiful | www.kab.org.au |
| | Nature Conservation Council of NSW | www.nccnsw.org.au |
| | Planet Ark | www.planetark.org |
| | Total Environment Centre | www.tec.org.au |
| | The Wilderness Society | www.wilderness.org.au |
| | WWF Australia | www.wwf.org.au |

## about Clean Up Australia

Clean Up Australia was founded in 1989 with the mission to Clean Up, Fix Up and Conserve the Environment. Clean Up Australia Day, held every year on the first Sunday in March, mobilises more than 750,000 volunteers at almost 800 sites nationally. Clean Up has also initiated and managed 'fix up' projects worth more than $30 million to tackle sources of pollution; conducts community and school education campaigns to reduce waste and create awareness about environmental issues; and since 1993 has exported the Australian initiative through the Clean Up the World campaign, run in conjunction with the United Nations Environment Programme (UNEP). More than 35 million volunteers in 120 countries are involved.

## we need your help

You can help either as a volunteer by giving your time, or by joining Clean Up Australia and making a regular contribution. All donations are tax deductable.

So, support Clean Up Australia's mission every day of the year by becoming a True Green Supporter. Go to www.cleanup.com.au/truegreen www. truegreen.org.au or call 1800 282 329

'For more than 16 years Clean Up Australia has empowered individuals to take care of our environment. The work of our volunteers has and will continue to make significant inroads, but now it's time to move to the next stage and address the significant environmental threats that face us today in the key areas of climate change, waste and water.'

Ian Kiernan, Clean Up Australia

Photograph: Marc Stanley, titomedia

## acknowledgements

Special thanks to Ian Kiernan for his inspiration, friendship, unstinting good humour and commitment to making a difference; Tim Wallace for his dedication, insight and creative editing, Marian Kyte for the inspired design; Lee McLachlan for image research; Katie Patrick of Green Pages Australia for her original research and advice; and Michelle Wood for her initial research.

The authors also wish to thank Brigitta Doyle from ABC Books, Margret Meagher, Jessamine Walker and John Cunningham.

Huge thanks also to the Clean Up Australia team for their assistance as well as dedication and commitment to protecting Australia's environment.

## authors

Kim McKay (right) is the co-founder and deputy chairwoman of Clean Up Australia and Clean Up the World. She is an international social marketing consultant who counts *National Geographic* among her clients.

Jenny Bonnin is a director of Clean Up Australia and Clean Up the World. She and Kim are partners in the social marketing firm Momentum2. Jenny has two children and lives with her partner and extended family.

'In Australia, we need to learn from the custom and culture of our Aboriginal people and tread lightly on the earth – in the belief that we don't own the land, we belong to it. It's up to us.'

Ian Kiernan, AO